Geraldine Taylor is a counsellor for students at Bristol University, and educational consultant to Penguin's birth-to-eight publishing team.

Her awards include BBC Wildlife Writer of the Year. Geraldine's latest wildlife book for children, *Why is the Sky Blue?* was chosen by the charity *Booktime* to give to all four year old children in England, in September 2010. The companion book, *Do Dogs Dream?* has won a *Right Start* gold award.

Dru Marland collaborated with Richard Beard on the acclaimed travel book and biography, *Becoming Drusilla*. She has illustrated several wildlife books and thinks that her pictures are getting better.

Contact Geraldine on: geraldine.taylor1@virgin.net
Dru on: drusilla.marland@btopenworld.com

THE CASE OF THE CURIOUS CROW

and other bird stories,
many mysterious

Geraldine Taylor

Illustrations by
Dru Marland

Eyeon Books
Bristol
2010

The Case of the Curious Crow
and other bird stories

Author: Geraldine Taylor
Published by: Eyeon Books
Design: Keith Taylor

Illustrations: Dru Marland
Tel: 0117 973 3575
Mob: 07977 125 824

Email: Drusilla.marland@btopenworld.com

ISBN 978-0-9551823-2-7

Eyeon Books
28, Berkeley Road, Bristol, BS6 7PJ
0117-973-2787

eyeon.books@virgin.net

Starlings

DEDICATION

Little egret

*I cannot even glance up and see a starling flying over
without a slight lift of the heart. I love the
independence of birds from man, and especially the
freedom that their powers of flight give them.*

*… When I watch them, I seem, in some way to live and
fly with them, also freed from my other human
preoccupations. I am happy to return to those, but
meanwhile birds have lifted me briefly into another
life.*

Derwent May: The Times Nature Diarist

Moonlight Bear

THE CASE OF THE CURIOUS CROW

and other bird stories, many mysterious

Yellow birds
Late April

I'm standing in Ashton Court Meadow at buttercup time - the eighth Wonder of the World. Skylarks rule here, pouring out their silver song, then falling from the sky, like drops of a Roman candle.

Skylarks land some way from their nest on the ground to mislead predators, and then dash to it under the cover of long grass. As these brown birds scuttle along, they are anointed with buttercup pollen. When I first saw the birds with yellow wings, I thought they were exotic songbirds, blown off-course. Then I looked down and saw that my old brown boots had turned to gold.

Overnight, badgers tread through buttercups, forging little there-and-back-again paths that radiate from their sett like the rays of the sun.

The black and white of these moonlight bears
wouldn't be brushed with yellow because
buttercup petals close at night to protect the
pollen. But I have seen rabbits here on a
buttercuppy morning, their fur sprinkled with
gold.

The dauntless dunnock
Mid-May – late June

There's always been a blackbird in my life.   The
current post holder is alarmist and opinionated,
but in song, he's Heaven's flute: eternity is in his
music. He lives in the holly tree under my
bedroom window, and our daily lives are woven
together from an early hour.

One morning, in the studied pauses in the
blackbird's song, the pauses he relies upon to let
the grandeur of his music impress itself upon the
air, and to hear the songs of other blackbirds,
there burst a sparkle of higher song, a river of
sweet notes.

An aria, followed by a bit of jolly rap.

The blackbird sang on, and the pop music
followed.

Who would dare to challenge the blackbird laureate like this?

The upstaged blackbird

Of all birds, it turned out to be a dunnock! A little brown job! From that morning, the blackbird was on alert, and the sight of the dunnock brought him hurtling out of his bush like Batman, dashing at the little bird, head like an arrow. There was no question of the dunnock using the birdbath, or perching on the fence.

But *still* the feisty little dunnock sprang up whenever the blackbird sang, and *still* he pitched his perky lyrics against the classic bravura of the blackbird. I held my breath when the pop song actually collided with the opera and the two birds sang together.

In late June, the blackbird's young fledged, and he stopped singing. Our rooftops were hushed. This was the opportunity the dunnock had been waiting for. He sung from the rooftops, the TV aerials, the lampposts and the church spire: those fast, triumphant notes - *Top of the world, made it Ma! Top of the world!*

The blackbird and the dunnock have since reconciled. They live with their mates in the holly tree. The dunnocks are too absorbed in each other to notice me. The blackbird, however, feigns high-minded independence and then shouts at me through the kitchen window when a cat appears.

An extravagant performance

My garden blackbird sings most powerfully when
his nestlings are a week or so out of the eggs: he
interrupts his food-bringing duties to launch into
an extravagant performance, usually in the middle
of the day and always close to his nest. It's as
though he's telling his nestlings what it is to be a
blackbird. Possibly, too, this reassures his mate
on the nest that all is well outside the bush.

Blackbirds are passionate parents; there's such
urgency in their coming and goings that
I long to muck in and help.

The phantom of the woods
May, Cotswolds

An inky intensity of bluebells, an orange-tip
butterfly on one of them, and a blackbird
skimming the surface of the blue like a swallow
over water. Suddenly, the birds stop in mid song,
and I look up to see why. Through the trees, as
though on a wire, glides a buzzard, not brushing
any branch: the phantom of the woods.

Buzzard in the woods (page 13)

The laughing thrush
April

The robins that welcome visitors to Observatory Hill in Clifton have been joined by a new attraction: a thrush has set himself up as a comedian. His repeated phrases, *I say, I say, I say …* are followed by wheezy chuckles as though the bird is creased up with laughter at his own jokes. Moreover, there is a certain ventriloquial quality to the bird and I am frequently looking for him up the wrong tree.

Raindrops keep falling …
May

Baby blue tits love the sun and they creep to the outside twigs of a bush, while inside, a parent bird, its call vibrating with anxiety, scolds them back to safety.

The hazel leaves above this baby blue tit are wet from recent rain and water drops keep falling on the bird's head. Rather than moving, the fluffy

yellow baby (scarcely bigger than a butterfly)
shakes itself and chirps merrily each time a drop
falls on it.

In the thick of things
Early May
Observatory Hill – 7.30 am

The air is dizzy with the songs of thrushes! On
this ash, a great tit is shouting *teacher teacher* so
urgently that it attracts an audience of small birds,
in the same way as they come from all directions
to mob a roosting owl. A male blackbird arrives
and the small birds scarper, but the blackbird
stays close to the great tit, listening.

 Songbirds take a professional interest in each
other's songs and many birds weave snatches of
others' songs into their own. A song thrush
nesting near this exuberant great tit has already
included *teacher teacher* in his repertoire.

Wood pigeons are particularly attracted to lively
singers, especially thrushes, robins, blackcaps and
chaffinches: they sit close by, paying attention.
Unlike songbirds, however, wood pigeons lack
the physical capacity to vary the content of their

own songs, but they like to be in the thick of
things, as I do.

*Even in the species songs by which we recognise
them, songbirds are not mechanical singers: they
are composers, virtuosos and professional
mimics. Their individual songs are variations on
their species theme, and these variations can
develop from year to year, influenced by other
birds, and sounds in the environment.*

*My garden blackbird, for example, now includes
a Mozartian warble, influenced, I am certain, by
the flute playing of Hannah, next door. A
vigorous and varied song is recognised by other
blackbirds as the mark of a healthy, desirable
mate.*

The goldfinch's apprentice

July is the quiet time for birds. I shut my eyes to
concentrate on any bits and pieces of birdsong.
There's a pretty song nearby: a mixture of
blackcap and dunnock, but rather too tinkerbelly
to be either.

I open my eyes to see a goldfinch on top of a
hawthorn, singing an intricate melody, a song
sampler. There's a baby goldfinch on the twig

Goldfinches

below it. The goldfinch flies to the sunlit top of
the next bush to sing there, and the fledgling
follows, bouncing through the air in its parent's
wing-beats, an eager apprentice.

*Young songbirds develop their species songs,
their public performances, in snatches, burbles
and cheeps, as the human infant babbles, coos
and imitates its way to language. Both birds and
humans need to hear the adult voice.*

The case of the curious crow
July

I wonder why this juvenile crow is taking so much trouble to establish himself in the middle of linden blossom? He has toppled twice already, but persists in attempting to balance on the bouncy end of a branch where there's a mass of flowers. Here he is again, his sooty head framed by fragrant, yellow flowers. God is in the detail.

Crows are masters of surveillance, absorbing everything around them in the search for something to their advantage: perhaps this crow wanted this unusual lookout point. The tenacity of this young bird echoes Aesop's fable of the *Crow and the Jug* in which the thirsty crow uses stones to raise the water level in a jug so he could drink. The moral of this tale is *where there's a will, there's a way.*

On the other hand, other Aesop's fables highlight the vanity of crows, so perhaps my linden blossom bird intended to frame himself to best advantage.

Additionally, young birds like perching on bouncing branches and crows are known for their playful personalities: perhaps this young bird was just larking about.

In 2009, scientists replicated the jug, water and stones situation with rooks (also members of the

Corvid family) and added the inducement of worms in the water. There is filmed evidence that the birds accurately raised the water height (thus getting the worms) using exactly the number of stones needed.

The blackberry spring

In the late summer, I creep around, putting my ear to bushes: fortunately it's the blackberry-picking season so this bushy loitering doesn't alarm onlookers.

At this time of year, birds hide in bushes to moult. Without a full complement of flight feathers, they are vulnerable to predators, so secrecy is the order of the day. Now and then, they utter exquisite sprigs of sound, their secret songs. Often, I hear robins practising their songs before returning to public life, with new feathers.

These intimate songs are known as *sub songs*. Possibly also, warm autumn spells cause the hormone level of the birds to rise, and they start to sing. I call this time *the blackberry spring* because rooks can be seen carrying nesting material around, and folk tell me that small birds fuss around garden nest boxes.

The blackberry spring ends with the first cold snap, and birds turn their attention to their food supply.

The starlight robin
October 5.30am

This silhouette of a little pudding in the moonlight is a robin. What a silvery trill! Folk often tell me that they have heard a nightingale locally, it *has* to be, no other song could be so beautiful. Later, they realise that they were standing, as I am now, thrilled by the song of a robin under the stars.

The autumn song is about establishing territory, and what we hear as beautiful is actually a sharp warning to other robins to keep out. Often, in the pauses between phrases, I can hear the songs of other robins far away.

Robins have large eyes and can see in the gloom.

Circus wagtails
October

Pied wagtails turn up in bleak places. They also stage appearances at cafés, car parks, and fairgrounds. Temporary buildings, stretches of mud and mesh fences, especially excite them.

These two wagtails are zigzagging around the circus caravans and look as though they are wired together in flight. Their song is an infectious giggle.

Aspects of pied wagtail behaviour puzzle me, especially their tendency to walk round and round lampposts. I have heard, though cannot personally confirm, that wagtails can become tame enough to touch. This apparently occurs near a food source, such as a café.

Rainbow gulls, and the hailstone fox
28th Nov 09 8.0 am

Thunder and lightning! Hail! A fox sitting on
Zoo Banks, head back, catching hailstones in its
mouth. Black sky, orange sun and a rainbow so
brightly enamelled that it seems impossible it
could ever fade. Gulls painted all colours of the
rainbow as they fly into it.

Herring gulls are observed to have seven
meanings to their different calls. I wonder what
they are calling now?

The beacon thrush
December
Bristol Downs: 7.30 am

I am lost in the fog. All is white and the trees
have gone.

I head for the yellow pinpricks of car headlights
but find it's not the road I expected. My plan is to
meet fellow birder Nick at our usual spot by the
Avon Gorge rocks. We have a code of honour to
turn up in all weathers, and I am making sad duck

Fox in Hailstorm (page 24)

noises in the hope that Nick will hear and answer me.

I pause to hear if Nick is making duck noises back. No, but the silence is now broken by a familiar song, a thrush. I know *exactly* which thrush and where he is singing.

Thrushes sing in mid winter to claim territories: this bird treats dog walkers and I to a concert in the early mornings, and performs three quarters of the way up the same ash tree.

I know this particular bird because his song incorporates verses of nuthatch call: interestingly, the thrush has territory in the woods where the nuthatches live. He's singing through the fog and I'm navigating not by the stars, but by a thrush.

The mystery singer
May

What *is* this bird? I'm lurking around this densely leaved holm oak listening to birdsong inside. The song can't be about territory, as few other birds would hear it; it must be a song to a mate.

Bullfinch in Sunbeam (page 28)

The bird's wistful, minor notes sound as though they are played on a scratched vinyl record. The oak is so dark inside that I can't see even the outline of the bird. I had hoped he would flit between trees and I could then identify this singer of love songs in the darkness.

December

Fellow birder Nick and I stagger across the Downs, against the most energetic of winds. On the top of this leafless ash is a male bullfinch, spot-lit by the sun to radiant rose pink, and calling, *psue psue.*

Do they have a song as well as that call? I ask Nick, who thinks not. Some bird authorities agree with him. Others mention the difficulty of hearing bullfinches actually *sing*, but confirm that they do.

Curiosity remaining, I check it on Internet birdsong sites, and discover that my holm oak singer is a bullfinch!

Bullfinches are secretive but the males cannot resist the sun; hence sudden encounters like this are possible.

The ice water robin
January

I look out of the bathroom window in the late afternoon as the light fades because this is when the robin sometimes arrives at the birdbath. I am about to get into a hot bath, and the robin is vigorously bobbing, ducking and fluffing in water that is all but ice-cold. Once, I broke the ice for him before I went upstairs.

Birds need to wash regularly to keep their feathers in good condition. This matters especially in winter as they fluff up their feathers to keep themselves warm.

The chaffinch story
July 25th

Small things because this is a small thing. A young female chaffinch flew into the Downs café yesterday, and this is what we did to help her get back outside.

Small things:
The little bird high in the rafters, then perching a bit lower and peering down at us.

Chris borrowing a green checked drying up cloth,
ready to catch her if she came near our table.
All windows impossible to open.
Us whistling to her and making bird noises, light-
hearted because we were sure it would end
happily.
Dru rushing home on her bike and returning with
two shrimping nets.
Every customer informed of the bird situation on
arrival.
Everyone looking up.
Here she comes, get ready ...
The awful silence when the little bird flew down
and smashed into the window.

The chaffinch

Smaller things:
The chaffinch carried outside in Chris's hand, her
beak wide open with shock.
The dark bruise on her head, the size of a 5p.
Her eyes closing, the bird ready to die.
Us talking to her and stroking her back to get her
to open her eyes again.
Our relief when she did.
Being unable to switch off my learning brain and
marvelling at the soft green wash of her back
feathers.
Not knowing what to do next.
Tucking her into a leaf-lined gutter.
Leaving her.
Making a little bird coffin out of a cake box in my
kitchen, ready for the next morning.
Memories of the past bird rescue failures.
Worrying all night.

More small things:
Getting up very early.
Reaching into the gutter of the café roof.
No stiff little bundle of feathers.
Customers asking about her, *is the bird all right?*
Chaffinches calling in the lime tree outside the
café.

Using the bird coffin to collect early blackberries.

A simpler life

In my previous book of bird stories, *The Coffee Thrush,* I offered to say more about birds and our happiness, if readers request it. Many have.

We want to love and feel beloved, and to have a life that means something. We need companions, to feel that we belong, and that we can contribute to others. We often wish we could live in a simpler way that reflects the things we most value. It would be good to feel some constancy against the waves of change.

Life is seldom straightforward, and events can derail us. We may lose people we loved and who gave us meaning. We make mistakes, and so do others: regret and worry can feel overwhelming. Also, I suspect the pace of change has seemed enormous to every generation.

It helps to look for the little things that cheer us. Sometimes even a brief episode of cheer shows our lives in a brighter light - so long as we do not dwell on sad things too quickly afterwards.

We can keep cheerful episodes alive, tell someone and revisit them in our minds. When I'm down, I think about the blue tits that use my birdbath. A more precious picture of kerfuffle and splash, it's hard to imagine; the memory makes me smile and feel more energetic.

We are uplifted by something to look forward to, by someone taking an interest in what interests us, by companionship and laughter, and by active engagement with the details of life, preferably outside.

Us birdwatchers need to talk about birds, and are keenly interested in what others have seen. Binoculars round my neck explain why I am loitering in woods, and admit me to any birder fellowship.

Being with birds is full of beautiful surprises and humour, and there are big birdy events to look forward to; for example, birds beginning to sing, nests being made, baby birds, and the return of the swifts (around 4th May).

There's simplicity about being with birds and I prefer to do this without fussing at something else – birds don't tick lists or use mobile phones. I rarely use my binoculars, as I'm content with what I see and hear.

For me, simplicity is spending time, empty-handed, with a bird, a wild animal, or a pet: this quietens my mind, and I feel full of love. I spent a while in the close company of a roe deer and I wrote about this in my book *Echolands*. Also, I have a beloved rabbit called Rosie who treats me with excited enthusiasm, as though she has just discovered me.

Loving birds offers some permanence in a world of change. My most exciting childhood discovery was the constancy of birds: I encountered the *same* birds on the same trees and bushes. I knew where and when to find blackbirds, and robins and thrushes! I'm a creature of habit and small territory myself, and so I know my birds and feel I'm among friends. When I'm indoors, I'm usually looking out of a window for birds, and was frequently told off for this at school.

My small territory sustains me on a daily basis and helps my life to work, despite the difficult times we all encounter.

We can get so bound up in our lives that we don't notice the astonishing loveliness around us. Sometimes, folk come birding with me and talk intently about their concerns … Hopefully the fresh air and exercise helped them, but they've walked past exquisite sights and songs that could have taken them out of themselves, and given their brain a lovely picture to keep.

Having read the story of the baby blackbird, *Chirrup,* in my previous book, people have asked how I can care deeply about individual birds when their lifespan is short, dodgy, and it will end in grief one way or the other. It seems to me that that is more of a reason to do it, not less. Of course we try to protect ourselves from grief and disappointment, but it could be that by doing so we insulate ourselves from great joy, and this has wider implications for the business of living.

The bald blackbird

15th July 7.0 am
Oh the scent of the linden blossom after the rain!
But what on earth is this by the elder bush? It's a
headless male blackbird. No, no – the poor bird
has a completely bald, white head. He looks like
a little skeleton in a black cloak. He's feeding on
the ground, along with chaffinches.

16th July 7.0 am
Checked up. Bald blackbird in same place.

17th July 7.0 am
Bald blackbird in usual place, and I creep nearer.
He's a strange sight, painful to my heart. I'm not
used to seeing blackbirds disadvantaged like this.
My blackbird bible (DW Snow) refers to the
*barish heads of juveniles, moulting to first year
plumage,* and talks about these birds having a
somewhat *vulturine* appearance. But this one
isn't barish or juvenile – he's an adult bird, and
utterly and startlingly bald.

19th July 7.0 am No blackbird.

Bald Blackbird

Every morning until August – nothing, no blackbird. Magpies in blackbird's place: worrying.

1st August 7.0 am
Looking for my bald blackbird, I run towards a black, crumpled object on the grass. But it's only a few blackened leaves.

3rd August 6.30 am
It's my blackbird! It has to be! He's in his usual place and his head is now patchily black! I'm so relieved.

From 3ʳᵈ August, until 23ʳᵈ January the next year, I did not see my bald blackbird, despite daily vigils. However ...

23rd January
What's this? It's my bald blackbird in his old place, and he's starkly bald again, and what's more, the baldness has spread to his neck.

My vigil continues but no luck.

9th February
Out late afternoon to post a letter, but divert to go in search of the bald blackbird for a second time today. Here's the green woodpecker ramming the

ground for ants, now looking up with that alert, head-back stance. No blackbird. I turn to walk home and suddenly the bald blackbird flies out of a hawthorn bush to the lowest branch of a beech. He's so conspicuous. I wait, and now he starts to sing, his bald head raised as though a skull is singing: a glorious fluting performance.

I forget to post the letter.

No more sightings

27th February
I've looked up bald blackbirds on the Internet, and found that a listener to BBC Radio 4 Home Planet has seen a bald thrush. Moreover the thrush became completely bald and died. The cause of this isn't known – it could be lice, feather mites or insufficient nutrients. This is also a phenomenon amongst blue jays in the USA and radio stations report that distressed listeners phone in to talk about what they've seen.

1 March
I'm riding on the front seat at the top of the bus and looking at the Downs. I see the bald blackbird with what appears to be a female blackbird. I run down the stairs and ask the bus driver to stop at once and let me off, but he says it

is more than his job is worth. I have to go to the next stop and run back. I want to make sure of what I saw. Too late. Gone.

I so badly want this blackbird to lead a normal life.

This happened in 2002/3 and despite months of vigils, I never saw the bald blackbird again.

In July 2009, the wildlife expert Simon King posted an item on the Internet about the bald blackbird he had seen, wondering if the baldness was a result of conflict between birds, or disease. That both of us had first encountered our bald blackbirds in the month of July suggests that the baldness is related to the bird's moult. However, my bald blackbird had not regained his head feathers by March of the following year, well into breeding season.

Field of Dreams
Ashton Court Meadow: 7.0 am Sunday 18th April 2010. All planes grounded by volcanic ash.

Frost, mist, skylarks, swallows, a crow showering in dewy grass, and willow warblers back on duty in all four corners of the meadow. I wonder if each has returned to the same corner as last year.

One willow warbler is singing at the same time as a blackcap - there's a moment at which it's impossible to separate the songs, and it's a duet from heaven.

Keith (husband) is with me today and says that as we walk through the meadow, it's closing down behind us: we're in a dream.

Skylark

For a second I wonder if that's true and I tell him I don't mind if it is – we're together. But I sneak a look behind me anyway, just to make sure.

It's not so much that the birdsong is sharper today, and I *like* planes, but maybe they stop the illusion of life being a dream. Today, the sky is glowing blue, and belongs only to the ups and downs and silvery sounds of skylarks in this playground of grace, this Camelot.

Willow warblers fly from West Africa to spend the summer here, and it's possible that these lovely little songbirds have flown 3,000 miles back to the same birch trees in the same corners of this meadow.

Postscript

Readers of my first bird storybook, *The Coffee Thrush*, ask me what has happened to the birds.

The Fairyland Thrush continues to sing in a minor key and this year, one of his phrases is a tumbling waterfall that gives me the shivers.

The Observatory Robins continue to welcome visitors.

The Coffee Thrush himself suffered a reverse when redwings and fieldfares invaded his holly tree outside the tearooms and stripped it of berries: he turns up now and then but no longer defends the tree.

I never saw *Marble* again.

Willow warblers sing and dance in all corners of the meadow at Ashton Court.

Blackbirds continue to address the nation.

All is well.

BIRDSONG TIMELINE

Learning about birdsong is a lifelong journey: speed is pointless

Male birds advertise themselves in their songs. It's mostly males that sing although female robins also sing. Birdsong is about mating and territory, although some song appears unaccountable. Experts are divided as to whether or not birds sometimes sing for the pleasure of it.

Song is largely a feature of the spring, and of dawn and dusk: at other times, birds are too busy nesting and feeding. The dawn chorus sounds to us a sharper, more urgent recital, and the evening chorus seems to reflect satisfaction at a day well done. These, though, are our emotions.

Bird calls are an instant reaction to what's happening around them, and along with their songs, are how they communicate with other birds.

The best way to identify birdsong is to see the bird, and hear the call or song at the same time, and then check its identity in a bird book. It's simplest to learn one song at a time, and starting early in the year helps this.

Song recordings are available, and you can check birdsong on some Internet sites

It helps to know what you are likely to hear and when you're likely to hear it, and this timeline will help. But with bird life, assume nothing. Birds are full of surprises.

MAIN SINGERS IN THE CENTRAL BRISTOL AREA

January

Wrens – sharp bursts
Mistle thrushes
Song thrushes early in morning
Dunnocks ruminating in bushes
Blue tits loud – often first singers of day
Great tits loud, all day
Ravens *pruking*
Nuthatches calling
Blackbirds singing early morning at end of month
Robins
Redwings

February
Mid-February - some dawn chorus

Dunnocks – often the soloists
Geenfinches
Blackbirds full song, and snatches, depending on weather
Song thrushes full song
Robins spring song
Chaffinch song – sometimes leaving out the final trill

Great tits even louder
Magpies
Jays
Resident skylarks over meadow areas
Woodpigeons call
Jackdaws noisy

March
More birds joining the dawn chorus

Nuthatches calling loudly
Great spotted woodpeckers drumming
Dunnocks
Goldfinches
Green woodpeckers laughing song
Blue tits
Over-wintering blackcaps start to sing
Coal tits
Chiffchaffs at end of March
Crows loud
Rooks
Blackbirds commanding full song
House sparrows
Starlings gather to sing and whistle
Goldcrests
Long-tailed tits
Collared doves
Treecreepers (very high pitched, as with
goldcrests, not everyone can hear them)

Greenfinches
Robins
Chaffinches with additional final flourish

April

Dawn chorus loud. Listen for individual birds in the chorus: I have heard a chorus apparently led by skylarks, and another led by a great tit. Thrushes, blackbirds and robins frequently lead. Crows and rooks provide the percussion.

Bullfinch (tree tops, especially in the sun)
Song thrush full song
Blackcaps
Dunnocks
Wrens alarm
Robins alarm
Great tits early morning
Willow warblers
Blackbirds now and then
Skylarks
Chiffchaffs
Swallows
Chaffinches loud
Greenfinches

May

Patchy dawn chorus. Periods of bird song silence.

Blackbirds – listen for evening performance
Thrushes
Blackcaps
House martins
Great tits
Willow warblers
Chaffinches loud
Chiffchaffs
Skylarks
Wrens
Swifts – listen for their screaming
Robins

June

Patchy dawn chorus
Birds sing if they still have youngsters to teach

Great tits
Song thrushes now and then
Robin – snatches
Chiffchaff – short episodes
Blackcap – short episodes
Blackbird – often sings in middle of day

Nuthatch snatches
Chaffinches sometimes sing all day
Magpies noisy
Starling babies noisy
Sparrows noisy

July
Many birds moulting

Chiffchaff episodes, with additional notes
Wren – startling bursts
Dunnock – pleasant songs now and then
Chaffinches – surprisingly frequent snatches
Greenfinches, the occasional wheeze
Blackbirds – as in June, often in the middle of the
day, sometimes at beginning, and dusk
Nuthatch calls
Blackcap – now and then
Peregrines – young noisy
Gulls

August
Birds moulting and concealed in bushes and trees

Collared doves calling in snatches
Magpies call and scold
Starlings gather, sing, whistle and wheeze
Dunnocks sing in snatches

Willow warbler – sudden mysterious snatches of
full song
Robins practise autumn song at end of month
Goldcrests high piping can be heard around Yew
trees

September

Dunnocks chatter in bushes and low trees
Robins sing and chink in bushes
Great tit snatches
Chiffchaff snatches
Wren snatches
Tantalising snatches of warblers as migrant birds
return home
Magpies
Jays noisy as they collect and bury acorns
Pied wagtails contact calls

Jay with acorn

October

Robins
Blue tits and great tits call
Long-tailed tits contact calls – one sings the first
part, the answering bird, the second
Blue tits
Great tits

November

Starlings gather in favourite trees, and click and
whistle
Wrens often sing in the morning (territories)
Blackbirds mutter in bushes, as do dunnocks.
Robins alarm call, and song
Song thrushes sing to establish territories
Jay calls
Mistle thrushes sing loudly on windy mornings
Redwings lovely sub song (we don't hear their
main song as in the spring, they fly back to
Scandinavia to nest)

December

Mistle thrushes
Song thrushes - especially mornings, even foggy

ones. Good time to learn the songs of individual
thrushes
Bullfinches
Great tits
Blue tits
Blackbird alarms
Ravens croaking
Robins – especially seasonal when sings in holly
bush
Redwings

Goldfinches

How to order from
EYEON BOOKS

(all prices include UK postage and packing)

Please send a cheque or postal order
made payable to:

Geraldine Taylor,
28, Berkeley Road
Westbury Park,
Bristol   BS6 7PJ

Tel: 0117 973 2787

Email: eyeon.books@virgin.net

EYE ON MAGAZINE

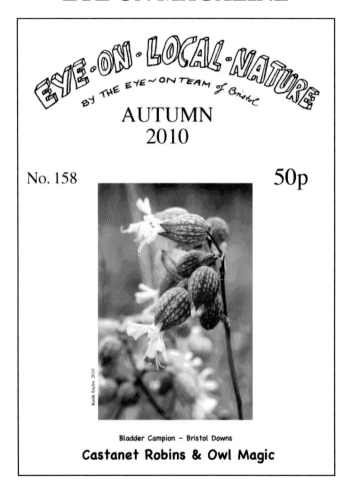

EYE·ON·LOCAL·NATURE

BY THE EYE~ON TEAM of Bristol

AUTUMN 2010

No. 158   50p

Bladder Campion – Bristol Downs

Castanet Robins & Owl Magic

Started in 1982, EYE ON Magazine keeps you in touch with what the birds, plants, animals and trees are doing, By post, quarterly: £3.00 for 4 issues, by cheque or PO, payable to G. Taylor, 28 Berkeley Rd, Bristol BS6 7PJ

"A delightful newsletter" The Times - 6 December 2008.

Other Books by Geraldine Taylor

ECHO LANDS – and other true tales of the Avon Gorge Woods

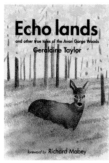

An extraordinary account by award winning author Geraldine Taylor, recording her experiences of twenty-first century woodlanding: early morning wanderings in the woods each day before work, open to whatever wildlife – and human – dramas come her way.

£3.00 Post free*

"Sparkling explorations" Richard Mabey, BBC Wildlife Magazine.

THE BRISTOL DOWNS – a natural history year

Geraldine Taylor's new book about the flora and fauna of the Downs. Each month, she gives two different walks with maps, and showcases the seasonal changes. With over 200 original drawings by Dru Marland to help identify the rich variety of plants, birds and other wildlife on the Downs. An ideal gift for all amateur naturalists and new wildlife watchers.

£6.50 Post free*

"Her own monthly diary with excellent notes." The Times - 6 December 2008.

* To order, send cheque or PO payable to G. Taylor to: Eyeon Books: 28, Berkeley Road, Bristol BS6 7PJ

GERALDINE'S FIRST BIRD BOOK

The Coffee Thrush – *£5.00* *(see page 54)*

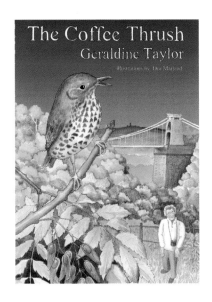

Geraldine and Coffee Thrush

Meet the Birds in the Band and the Observatory Robins!

Long-tailed tits tumble

The local alpha
male Blackbird

Chirrup the
injured fledgling

Thrush and
admirers

Talks by Keith Taylor

1. Wildflowers of the Avon Gorge

2. The Cotswold Wildflower Show

3. *Coming soon – The romance of flowers*

Over 100 high quality colour slides in close-up of the rare, the beautiful and the bizarre plants that grow in Bristol, Somerset and Gloucestershire.

Entertaining and informative.

Keith's work has been featured in BBC Wildlife Magazine. He is a past president of Bristol Speakers.

To Book, phone: 0117 973 2787 or Email: Eyeon.books@virgin.net

Pictures by Keith Taylor

Beautiful hand made pictures in frameless mounts, selected from Keith's best wildlife photographs. Make ideal presents. Freestanding if required. Selection of 12 flowers and butterflies. Size A5 approx. £2.50 each post paid.

For details, phone: 0117 973 2787 or Email: eyeon.books@virgin.net

Dru Pictures

commissions undertaken for books, portraits, and illustrations.

drusilla.marland@btopenworld.com

0117 9733575